I MAKE YOU BIRD

Diana Cant is a poet and child psychotherapist, living in rural Kent. Her poems have been published in various anthologies and magazines, including *Agenda, The North,* and *Poetry News*. She has published two previous pamphlets, *Student Bodies, 1968,* and *At Risk – the lives some children live*, and was voted Canterbury Peoples' Poet in 2020. She was nominated for the Forward Prize for best individual poem, 2023, and is the winner of the Plaza Poetry Prize, 2023. She is a joint editor of *The Alchemy Spoon*.

Also by AUTHOR NAME

At Risk (Vole Books, 2021)

Student Bodies 1968 (Clayhanger Press, 2020)

PRAISE for *I Make You Bird*

Though Diana Cant's vivid and encompassing *I Make You Bird* is ostensibly a book of elegy, it chronicles love and loss with such metaphorical reach that its form is really spiral: the beloved is gone, but the love is back, beginning, re-beginning in every poem. Home and garden sprout such joy and melancholy that we seem to be on a slowly turning planet, neighbourly, consoling, where the claims of dream and delight more than match the claims of time.

  — Glyn Maxwell

Diana Cant is a poet who has written with great compassion and care about fragile and difficult lives. Now she turns her attention to the pain of losing a long-term partner to a terminal illness – a tough subject she faces with characteristic openness and generosity. *I Make You Bird* is a soaring collection charting the path of grief and rebirth, and a beautiful and eloquent testament to how we hold those we love in our hearts – even when they are no longer present.

  — Tamar Yoseloff

It takes courage to hold onto living in the face of dying. Those of us who work and struggle with the impossibilities of grief in the aftermath of traumatic loss might make more space for the power of poetry, the imagination and our ordinary, human need to find aesthetic expression in the search for ways to bear the unbearable.

  — Maggie Schaedel

For John

I am living. I remember you.
— Marie Howe, *What the living do*

ISBN: 978-1-916938-46-5

The author has asserted their right to be identified as the author of this Work in accordance with the Copyright, Designs and Patents Act 1988

Cover designed by Aaron Kent

Edited and Typeset by Aaron Kent

Broken Sleep Books Ltd
PO BOX 102
Llandysul
SA44 9BG

CONTENTS

I Make You Bird

Diana Cant

Broken Sleep Books

FAMILY GROUP

(working drawing/pastel)

propped against your easel
a photo of the four of us
in black and white   perched
awkwardly on a garden seat
when our sons were young

in your hands our bodies rise
to meet you   our limbs are
disconnected   reassembled
you distil the greyscale image
extract our elemental shapes

vivid colour floods the page
as you tempt us into life
greens twist as yellows jostle
gentle blues   pinks   oranges
rough and tumble   a fine red
threads its way throughout

our bodies arc and curve
together   the rainbow reach
of your imagination
restores us to ourselves
unites us all

THAT THING CALLED LOVE...

it wasn't that the earth moved, seismic beneath my feet
or that my life lit up, rosy-glowed before my eyes,

it wasn't that I couldn't get to sleep that night, or that my mind
filled with every cliché in the book,

it wasn't that I was dumbstruck, tongue-tied, stupefied
or that my stomach somersaulted in delight,

it wasn't as if your words fell as music to my waiting ears
and sang like nightingales to me,

it wasn't that I remembered with obsessive clarity every
stitch of clothing that you wore,

it wasn't even that I fancied the pants off you and couldn't wait
to get you into bed,

no, I'm pretty sure it was none of that; what clinched it was
you bought me fish and chips.

CARRION CROW

I hate the way pain marches on your body like a carrion crow,
the way your eyes cloud as you try to rise above it,
the way it steals you from me, picking at your entrails:
it robs us.

Yet on those days when crow sleeps, or is busy elsewhere in the world,
we have some ease, the ease of eagles on a thermal, catching time;
we build ourselves a raft of timbers, notched with ancient marks:
we set sail.

Too far from shore for crow to reach us, we sing songs
from the heartwood of our ancestors, those early carpenters
who carved talismans to protect us from crow's scheming eye:
we are revived.

BOWERBIRD

The woods are dank, rain hangs in leaf-spaces
and wolf-winter prowls behind the trees.

At dusk we meet him face-to-face, his eyes
unblinking as he circles our fledgling home.

When we were young you were a bowerbird, bringing
bright trinkets, furnishing your nest with emerald delights,

vermillion feathers; a tail, a lustrous coxcomb
and I was won, drawn to your sequin shimmer

to a life that promised dance-steps in full costume,
a cloak of colours to set against the gloom.

Wolf beware! – you have not claimed us yet;
we will build a bower against the night

and you will howl in vain.

BIOPSY

I know you dread
words of confirmation.
I know you didn't sleep,
paced the house, disturbed the dogs,
confused them into thinking
time was altered:
how I wish.

The hospital again,
heart-sink smell
of disinfectant,
fluctuating tedium
of a waiting room,
the nurse's roll-call,
the daily list.

You, in my blue and white kimono,
slippers taken
from a holiday hotel,
nurse-led, disappearing
down a corridor;
breathe,
I've got your back.

Time passes quietly
a soap-blown bubble:
you reappear, stretchered
through double doors,

waving.
I breathe,
hello my love,
you're back.

DIAGNOSIS

Since the phone-call
we've been careful with each other,
treading our way
through thorn and thicket,
foot-dragging towards
a bitter truth.

We drive slowly down
the valley into the glare
of the motorway;
the car-speed and horn-blare
frighten us and we flinch.
If we make ourselves
so very small
we may escape.

At last, a turning,
a well-worn threshold,
the smell of roast lamb,
rosemary, gravy
and the comfort of potatoes

our sons, their arms outstretched.

DIDO AND AENEAS

we knew by then
this was always
a lament we loved

sadness soaring
elegiac above Carthage
a timeless fate

you hold my hand
in the cold concert hall
and we rise beyond

our rich remembering
driving home
your hand is chilled

PAPER CRANES

We lie here, folded,
forgotten by the world
smiling in the half-light;
the origami shapes
of our belonging
form pleated birds
full of promise
and fragility.
Such unexpected ease,
I rest my head on your chest
and we breathe
the magnetic pull
of our small earth's core.

HUSBANDRY

I'm pruning roses, cutting out dead wood.
Stop! commands the sun, *sit and look!*
she grabs me by the hand, makes me rest – true,
the gin and tonic helps, but mostly it's her warmth.

I pay attention to what attention brings:
hear the pregnant ewes close-cropping turf,
watch the dog's nose twitch, some rich language
like the bee's dance, unknown to me.
I smell engine oil and new-mown grass,
sink into the blowsy bosom of the heat.

I see you cross the garden, spade in hand,
I call out *two gin and tonics and I'm anyone's*,
wait – because of course you come, hold me, laugh,
as we discuss where to plant the roses for next year.

WOLF'S BANE

I've been uncovering aconites, yellow heads
bowed beneath a greatcoat of last year's leaves,
their stems sickly, in need of light.
Last autumn's weight lies heavy, as I free them,
help them tip their pallid faces to the sun;
an autumn of grim gatherings, of hijacked time,
a world gone mad, or bad, or both.
We're all of us in need of sun.

Look, I say, *the aconites are back,*
and although I know how much you love them,
how you watch for them each year,
how they're a proof of something,
as you kneel to see their mortal beauty
I'm ambushed by your sudden tears.

RUST

Ground bruise-blackened,
soil hard-worked, furrowed,
iron on stone, scars of toil
on thin-skinned earth.

Two rusting ploughshares
pockmarked and pitted,
red ferric crumbling
of an old horseshoe.

Hidden in the brush,
an injured fox cub,
paw slashed on flint,
russet-red, alone.

How is it that a body rusts?
An overnight bruise,
a skin too thin, no longer
stirring to the touch.

ALL THIS

After a long night in the war-torn territory
of pain, where all roads run to ruin
with a shell-shocked face,
after the dark mercenary hours,
your legs buckling, breath rasping,
and we two,
walled-in by fear,
helpless to help,
to find the panic-room door;
finally the warm flash of emergency lights,
the oh-so-welcome blare of blues-and-twos,
and Paul and Dave, sitting high,
comfortably padded in green uniforms -
just a minute, love, we'll get the kit,
and so much kit,
monitors bleeping,
readings, trailing leads,
technology spewing paper trails,
and these men,
kneeling, feeling pulse and tremor,
joking at their own expense to make us smile –
Dave here's dyslexic, that's why I give him
all the writing, c'mon, Dave, keep up -
as Dave regales us with the time he nearly died,
mashed-up in a motor-bike disaster,
a disaster that made him do
what he does now;
all this

and isolation shrinks, panic diminishes,
as we ride the rain-washed roads
with two men who carry you safely,
who take your pain gently
through dawn streets,
and Paul says,
you were right to call.

INTRAVENOUS

i

this drip, drip of yew
and periwinkle, docetaxel,
sounding soft and tactile
pillowing attack, a fine line
shooting a vein
hard plastic iridescence

ii

toxins sap your blood
to make you whole

so your fragile bones may bend
with the suppleness of willow

instead of breaking
with the splintering hardness of yew

a sapling army
a sword cutting deep

no way out but through
skin   organ   bone

iii

you sleep yourself away from me
down furrowed pathways
bone-tired
your body channelled out
by slippered assassins
crowing at day-break

HAIR

today there is hair
in the basin
and on your brush
thin grey threads
dropped as if
to map a way back

skin pale as milk-sop
tiredness so vast
no mother's arms
could hold it

your long black hair
tied back
a life-time ago

CAESURA

I find you stretched
on the old leather sofa
sleeping slowly

your face clear
unetched
your body turning
with an unnatural tide

your patient dog
curled like a comma
paused at your feet

DYING FOR AUTUMN

You worry at the death
of small winged things
dying for autumn

the dragonfly, green iridescence
on a flower stem,
blue eyes burning

wings alive with tracery
her shrunken abdomen
with no more eggs to give

the dark red admiral, flutter-slow
and wavering, seeking hibernation
before the weather turns

the greenfinch espaliered
against a window
flying as the sun is low.

You rescue them, of course you do,
take them gently on your finger,
watch them cling

as if their lives depend on you.
Perhaps they do.
I hardly like to tell you of the bird

the dog laid at my feet today
mouth-gentled and feather-damp,
red-legged, eyes glassy

caught before her time was due.
I rescue her, of course I do,
set her free for you.

LEPUS ARCTICUS

Your white shadow
falls across the winter moon,
wrong-footing my senses.

In China they believe
you pound base minerals
of the moon's silver backbone

to make the elixir of immortality.
I would plead for that;
not for myself, but for another

who would need
the merest drop
to stop the tread of time.

YEAR END

We are safely gathered in, a net cast wide.
Our sons arrive, trailing comet tails
studded with the year's occasions, bright beads
threaded on the annual abacus, a tally to be reckoned,
added to the sum of things, the sum of us.
The house sleeps: our boys still lodged
in childhood beds, now surfing different dreams.
We two listen to the quietness
and whisper *the house is full again*,
breathing with more rhythms than our own.
In those moments, lying listening-close,
when we might doubt the record, we count
the beads and murmur to each other
we did this well.

INHERITANCE

Your pledge of gardening time, written
on an old receipt, hangs in the kitchen,
a promise you redeem. Wooden garden steps
grown rotten with the years, and you,
a son who watched and learned your way
around the saw, the jemmy and the mallet,
hack out old railway sleepers drenched in tar,
mark and cut new Douglas fir, drive wedge
to wood with certainty, until the steps are safe.

Later, we burn ash and birch, drink whisky,
reminisce –those conkers you took to school
years ago, bright offerings of friendship:
a sudden smile ignites your face – your father's,
now grown gloriously your own.

WHITTLE

You visit us with gifts – whisky,
a bottle of prosecco, flowers –
bestowed with cheerful generosity;
you update us, our horizons lengthen,
you upload us into modern life.
You offer us a twist to our old certainties,
kaleidoscopic pieces shaken
into different diamond shapes;
how did that rowdy, wayward child
– all that *boyness* – come to this,
the confidence of manhood
lodged firm beneath your skin.

By the fire light you whittle us
a wooden spoon, pale blonde curls
of beech lie scattered on the floor
like petals, like confetti.

SMALL ADJUSTMENTS

We buried her yesterday,
in a corner of the garden, beneath a tree,
curled in a blanket as if she was asleep.
You, your face wet, radiant with loss and love,
feeling the hollow that bounty leaves behind.

The younger dog walks more slowly now,
as if she has imported weight and gravitas.
These small adjustments to the pace of things,
these gradual increments of grief.

We hold each other in the evening air,
aware each death is a rehearsal,
remembering her glad and easy grace:
how simply we slide from the core of things,
how quietly we drop from life.

CHRYSALIS

June days, when light should idle
and sun should loiter;
instead, rain –
the ordinary drip of time,
dull, dismal.

While you dream away the drugged hours
I conjure up the minstrel you,
dancing to Praetorius,
our eyrie over Portobello Road,
the sun-soaked flower-beds
of Love-Lies-Bleeding
seeding in the wind.

Limbs frail as butterflies,
parchment-thin and paper-white,
antennae uncurling, filigree
fingering the eddying air;
a day-time shimmer
not the night-time brush
of mothy wings.

You feel your way towards unfolding,
I hold my breath –
dare to hope
you'll wake restored
to fly again.

BIRDMAN

I make you bird:
you arrive in different guises,
each bright-billed and wind-ruffled –

a feathered native, dark and querulous,
a rook, a raven; or something more exotic
flying in from steamy rainforest –

my birdman lover,
my bird of paradise,
my homespun blackbird.

Today I hold your fledgling head
eggshell-fragile and baby-bald,
sun-vulnerable

your bones shiver
as they feel their strength return,
migration on their mind –

it is summer
and you are recovering:
stay.

GRADUATION

after the festivities
the nightmare journey
that cost you dear

we rest at our hotel
toast our achievement
drink to us

your smile bone-tired
exultant
blushed by love

THE HOURS

Lauds, the dawn chorus,
and at last you sink
to deeper sleep,
your breath quieter now
your body still

blackbird and wren
pipe in the morning
birds quiver in the hawthorn,
swags of froth, wreaths of white,
leaf-tracery unseen
through the dark hours,
Compline, Vigil,

as the sun reaches Prime,
a maple flares
the meridian of the day
you sleep away
the noontime hours,
Terce slips to Sext
drifts to Nones;

the birds quiet now,
busy with the work of living;
the sun slides to the west
sounds are echo-muffled

you wake for Vespers
with the dusk,
to a cloistered sky
and one small owl,
ready to start
another night's crusade

TO MANAGE PAIN WE ALL DISSEMBLE; TO MANAGE MORTAL PAIN WE CONFABULATE

Your heavy-duty opioid use is seeping under all our skins. We never quite know where to find you; each morning drifts you to a different shore, leaves you bellied-up, beached, wearing that small boy's stare as you try to work out where you are today. Yesterday we found you down in Tennessee, with Little Richard, two ol' boys, showing how it's done. Another dawn we discovered you hiding in the Hindu Kush, waiting until morning to cross the border, poppies and the scent of danger in long grass. Next, you were in Blackpool, cooking a full English for thirty-eight. Two days ago a TV newsreader spoke to you directly, demanding you march north *with other cases like you,* outcast, unclean. You begged us not to let you go, a child's terror trembling in your face. We used to panic. Now we try to laugh. This morning it was Finland – but we're learning, we didn't ask – made you tea and toast until the moment passed. We make you into our brave adventurer, teller of tall tales, slayer of dragons, vanquisher of midnight monsters underneath the bed. *I don't know how to get this right,* you said.

ANNIVERSARY

Thirty-seven years since we stood beaming on Finsbury Town Hall steps
(we had wanted its' Art Deco facade so we'd faked a friend's address);

those were the days it was bourgeois to wear wedding white,
so, you in pink and me in blue; we felt the prize-winners we truly were;

one son growing well inside, another to come later – our family,
with all the world ahead of us. And it proved true; loving you

was the best choice I have ever made; your kindness, your generosity
the bedrock of it all. Forty-nine years ago, when we met,

you danced to Pretorius, in an upstairs flat on Portobello Road
with a leaping joy you carry still: I love you still.

THE BED

When the bed arrived we took against it, unwelcome guest,
unyielding metal frame, flashing pump to keep the mattress up.

The man said he'd come back each year to service it – we laughed,
believing three months and you'd be leaping upstairs again

once the chemo had done its stuff. We tried to humanise it,
dressed it in cheerful colours, pictures of swallows flying south to the sun

but there wasn't room for both of us, so sometimes we took turns,
me on the bed, you on the baggy yellow settee.

We installed a large tv and you discovered videos of people walking,
no sound except the reassuring tramp of someone else's feet.

We watched and walked for miles – canal towpaths were the best,
Bow Creek, the Hertford Union, Limehouse Cut.

We began to know their faces – the woman with her dog,
the man feeding pigeons, the children on their bikes,

to feel the comfort of what we could predict;
the bed became a narrowboat, waiting resolutely at each lock.

One long, hard night we walked the River Lee deep into the country
where you were born, and that was difficult, so much had changed.

And when the big pain came, you told me to go,
wanting to walk the London streets alone.

I came down next morning to find you propped up, sleeping
to the heartbeat of a stranger's feet.

Then the day your narrowboat had disappeared,
no engine chug, no steady towpath steps, no flashing pump.

The bed deflated and dismantled. The same man came to take it back.

WREN

I see you, but you're not there,
in the bird-pierced early dawn
I enfold you, but hold empty air.

Dew has pooled in your footprints
where you walked the old drove road,
I see you, but you're not there.

Stepping gallantly towards clear morning
taking nothing with you but the night,
I enfold you, but hold empty air.

Take her with you, I call out, urgent –
in my hands a small bright wren,
I see you, but you're not there

and although you do not take her,
she flies from me, darting to your side.
I enfold you, but hold empty air.

The loudest song bursts
from the smallest heart;
I see you, but you're not there,
I enfold you, but hold empty air.

DRIFT

Spin me a tale from time ago,
    a tale before uncertainty and a lowered sky;
weave me a story, thread-rich, capacious,
    strung with river-murmur and spawning salmon;
riddle me the old ways, weighty, eternal,
    the sun's retreat, the menace of the moon;
as a white owl slips through the dark cleft of night,
    sing me a keening song, a song of remembering
and I will hold my breath,
    stretch my arms to catch you as you glide past,
your eyes translucent, your body blurred,
    drifting in your slipstream
far beyond my reach.

REVENUE

Today the Inland Revenue contacted me
to say you have more tax to pay.
How many times must I tell them
you're dead?

I walk the long way round the lane
to shake them from my head.
Someone has inked a curved red heart
on the first tree of the wood
where old man's beard has tangled
with orange hips and haws.
The buzzard chicks have fledged,
their parents circle anxiously
to protect them from the crows.
At my feet, a slow-worm,
green gold, sun-basking
on the path, carves out arcs,
fast figures of eight as it escapes
to ivy cover.

In the leaf litter, a jay's wing feather,
bright bars of blue and black, wealth
I could offer to the Revenue
if they could see its' worth.

RUBBISH

My phone pings – a reminder
to put out the bins –
your IT legacy
and I'm glad of it.
Trundling down the drive,
next-door's dog on high alert,
I feel how light
these bins are now,
not the laboured trudge
they were. We've had longer
rougher drives, houses
further off the beaten track.
What was it my neighbour
called his dog? *Jaunty* –
such a good word, cheerful,
eager into life. *Russet* –
another trusty word,
your favourite apple, good
like *rubbish,* come to think of it,
especially if it's an adjective.
How much rubbish
does a person make,
two twice as much as one?
The difference seems significant.
I wonder, do the bin-men
sense the lighter load?

THE LOG-MAN COMES AND WE MIS-SPEAK

The log-man comes, first person I've seen
all week, truck full of seasoned ash.
Leaps from his cab,
where d'you want it, love?
a wolfish grin. I gesture to the wood-shed,
cut the banter dead.
Undeterred he tries again,
how you managing lockdown, love?
Ahh - a lockdown conversation,
well, I might be up for that.
I thaw, mention dog-walks in the wood.
Mistake.
Bet you're the Labrador type,
obedient-like.
 I bat it back – does he have dogs?
Two Jack Russells, little buggers,
don't like my dogs too willing,
nor my women – the ex-wife's Brazilian,
no way she'd do what she was told.
Oh God, this isn't good.
But now I see a softness in his face,
regret as he talks about his wife.
He tells me he hasn't always done this job,
used to live in Norfolk, like me. Locked
in the pleasure of remembering,
 – how did we come to this? –
we're talking about rejection,
how hard it is to bear. He says

he tells his teenage son
managing rejection's a lesson best learnt young.
He pulls a lever, logs spill out,
a satisfying clatter, a store of warmth.
From the cab waves a large hand
and he's gone.
One and a half tonnes of wood,
two hours of stacking.
This'll last me for weeks.

MILESTONE

A change of car, another marker,
a transit towards the sensible;
after many years, my sporty love,
throaty and convertible,
has come to grief,
but unlike you,
can be replaced.

I run the gauntlet of the used-car salesman,
Call me Steve, he announces sinuously
behind his lockdown mask;
brown pointed shoes, too shiny to be leather,
blue suit and tie, a grubby collar,
the uniform of car-persuasion.

I set out my four demands,
he has three cars that fit,
I pick one – job done.
I wonder, if you were here,
would we have done things differently?
I doubt it.
We always bought our cars this way,

THE DAY THE BOILER DIED...

and all electrics fuse, at the low point of the year,
and I dread cold, am seized by primitive anxiety.
At last, some help arrives– Liam, master craftsman,

new boiler in his van – *three days, love, we'll sort you out.*
Relief floods through me as he works and I bring tea,
he tells me he has allergies and can't drink milk,

that his mother died recently and how sad he feels –
a bit of a mother's boy, he calls himself,
with love and with regret. The next day he brings his dad,

to help with all the lifting; taciturn and sadder still,
talking quietly to the dog. Liam whispers
he's just had his dog put down. The lives of others,

the lives of all of us, the loss and going-on.
Day three, we have heat and light and I'm elated,
Liam and his dad confess that they'd been anxious too,

worried the job might prove too much for them
in their depleted state; the boiler hums reliably,
we wish each other luck, they leave a guarantee.

THE OLD WAY

A buzzard swoops as close as breath
wingtips whisper a roost nearby

two lime-green butterflies flit
between ramson and herb robert
marbled in the sun

yellow from the cowslip field
the dog rolls in the dandelions

piss-a-bed, we children said,
like that would stop us picking them
and blowing time away.

We found this drove-way years ago
in winter, when the branches arched

a tunnel overhead, and snow
had carpeted a path invisible
until then.

White windflower stars, proud
proclamation of a purple orchid

moss a prehistoric sea of green
pierced by witches' thimbles, trembling
violet blue.

Two years ago you said
the canopy of the wood was lifting

opening, letting in the light.
I couldn't see it then and doubted you;
I see it now.

LATE CUCKOO

Low thunder rumbles, the sky
is leaden, the woods dank, leaves hang
lifeless and for a moment I'm afraid.
Cleaver smothers end-of-season bluebells,
purple orchids buckle at the knee,
everything is that dull green that signals
spring is coming to an end.
In the distance a late cuckoo,
monotonous, insistent.

I took some clothes to the charity shop today,
checked my breasts for cancer
knowing the statistic is one in two,
did some weeding, walked the dog,
Almost a year without you.

IT OFTEN SNOWS IN APRIL

usually
when I switch off the lights
pull the curtains and go upstairs to bed
the dog turns tail and vanishes
to landscapes of her own

but lately
as nights are colder
and the bed is empty
she reappears, moving quietly
so as not to wake me
settling at my feet

then
last night as I dreamed of you
laughing halfway up a mountain
in unexpected snow, she barked
into midnight darkness,
shocking my sleeping self
robbing me of you

AFTER MUCH RAIN...

I venture out with the dog;
    exposed in the aftermath
        scattered petals of the last rose,
        an upturned mushroom with gills of palest pink,
        the soft underbelly of a vole,

and still the skylarks sing, so late in the year;
the morning hills look welcoming,
            low sun,
                long autumn shadows across ploughed fields,

the buzzards are out in force,
    they wheel and glide, guiding me
        along the tilled earth's edge;

rain haze in the distance, and although it threatens,
I have hope I may reach home before it breaks;
    the dog, bedraggled from her excavations in the hedge,
        presses her nose towards the west;

home again,
    I rediscover the delight of dropping
        my coat carelessly on the floor as I come in,
            child-like, but now with no-one to pick it up,
        to right the sleeves from inside-out.

GRANDSON

You'd have drawn such joy from this,
you'd have blazed canary yellow with the sun;

you'd have seized the laughing child and danced
that gladsome dance that only you could do.

Kidnapper for a day, you'd have leapt towards
the mellow sky, lingered among gold-finned clouds,

waded through saffron water to build a bed
on flaxen hills. But when night had elbowed in, edgy

with sharp insistence, and yellow bled to black,
you'd have returned your tiny passenger, wrapped

in glowing spider webs, and placed him gently back
into the living arms of his newly waiting world.

IN WHICH I WAKE YOU FROM YOUR SLEEP IN A DRAWER

You've come to stay, all six months of you,
smelling of skin and milk and biscuit. And your parents
have left you, having important things to do,

left you in my anxious care. They've left you sleeping
in a wooden drawer – there were extenuating circumstances,
and babies have slept in drawers for centuries

and besides you fit so well. I have instructions to wake you
if you sleep too long, change you, feed you, but
what is too long and who am I to judge?

Two hours, and your time is up, time to haul you
back to shore. I creep in. You're nonchalant in your sleep,
one arm draped casually over the drawer' edge.

I hesitate – you don't know me well and I've never
woken you before; you may panic, cry as if your world
is ending and how would we row back from there?

I kneel, quietly call your name. Surfacing, your eyes swim
me into focus – a pause, a look of puzzlement, then
your whole body becomes a smile – face, arms, legs

and we are beaming, and the beam becomes a laugh
and the laugh becomes a song until we're singing – timeless,
unwavering, and I know again what it means to fall in love.

EATING SEAFOOD IN MARGATE

Some days, when clouds are down
        and the morning seems it will never meet the sun,
I sit in bed,
    first cup of coffee in my hand
        and wish I could allow the news to go unread.

Some days, when birdsong is in short supply
        and even the dog has forsaken dreams
            of gamebirds held softly in the mouth,
I am slow to dress and breakfast
        and fail to reassure myself that the worst has passed.

Six new-laid eggs
    left on my doorstep,
        freckle-faced and nesting in their cardboard,
            some with feathers still attached;
                a gift,
                an act of kindness from a neighbour
                    to tempt my appetite.
                    I know these hens,
                the field they peck at in the daytime,
            the coop they roost in overnight,
        they live a good life, as far as hens' lives go,
    as far as I can tell.

Days pass.

Impromptu lunch with a friend, sitting in a bar, windows steamed
against the rain, eating seafood where the young ones are;
small, crafted plates –

    translucent oysters sliding from their shells,

        brown shrimps with broccoli and chilli,

            mackerel gleaming with nasturtium flowers,

            the kitchen heat, the buzz of speech

and I feel giddy,

    in the swing of things,

        a sharp excitement that it's not too late.

THROW THOSE CURTAINS WIDE *

You're outside, early doors, with the rising sun
making sure the gazebo is assembled right,
ready to house the drinks for later; you're there
supervising the putting-out of chairs, those deckchairs
that collapse if you get the geometry wrong. Earlier,
as I'd tried to make your legendary cheesecake
and forgot the baking powder, - *it'll still be fine,*
you'd laughed. You're with us as we dash to Tesco's
for more ice for the champagne, and you see us worry
about the late arrival of Dan, the hog-roast man.

When finally the guests arrive, you're everywhere,
partygoer head to toe, chatting on the garden benches,
in the studio amongst your sculptures, your image
on the screen. Quiet and thoughtful through the speeches
while the dog explores discarded plates, gathering
pork gleanings. You pay attention as everyone pays tribute –
as they remember your kindness, how much they loved you,
how much you made them laugh – we raise a glass.
Later, as people leave, your name lives in the air;

the sun had shone the whole day through – strange
how much that mattered. And then it was afterwards,
and the only person missing was you.

*from the song, *One day like this,* by Elbow.

62

THREE YEARS ON

Outside,
    the chairs wear updated sage-green cushions,
    bronze fennel tangles with French roses,
    an overflow of wood pigeons flaps clumsily from tree to tree,
        the talk is of allotments
            and the best time to sow runner beans.

You would have smiled
to hear your children moving
into gardening so seamlessly;
    hope may be the alchemy that's setting this day free.

Inside now,
    the family is cooking up a lunch-time storm,
    recipes collide as everybody makes what they do best,
        sequinned pink salmon sidles up to purple beetroot,
            yellow sweetcorn flirts with acid lime,
                blue cheese and walnuts dance with clementines.

We don't talk about you much;
    someone sets the table,
    someone carves and someone pours,
        it all gets done without the need for words.
And honestly,
    how comforting it is to be without the words,
    to be untethered, unconfined,
        as if the day can be trusted to take care of itself.

We drift outside again.
    Overhead,
    the sky a perfect blue,
    a small plane cuts its engine, falls silent,
    coughs, restarts.

SEEDING

a day spent weeding
faded forget-me-nots

as if I would.

ACKNOWLEDGEMENTS

My thanks are due to the editors of the following magazines and anthologies where several of these poems first appeared:
Agenda; Brittle Star; Finished Creatures; Poetry News; The Alchemy Spoon; The North; and the *Ver, Write Out Loud* and *Plaza Prize* anthologies.

Thank you also to Tamar Yoseloff, Glyn Maxwell and Jacqueline Saphra who have all, in various ways, played an important part in the making of these poems. To the members of the Canada Water Group, the Sage Poetry Group, and the Mid Kent Stanza Group — thank you all. An especial thank you to my Tercet friends, Judith Wozniac and Vanessa Lampert, who have seen me, and these poems through many changes, with loyalty and good humour.

My sincere thanks to Aaron Kent and the team at Broken Sleep Books for believing in these poems.

And finally, of course, to my extraordinary family and close friends, all of whom have given me more than I can ever describe or repay.

LAY OUT YOUR UNREST

Printed in the USA
CPSIA information can be obtained
at www.ICGtesting.com
CBHW030233150924
14303CB00004B/113

9 781916 938465